LEEDS TRANSPORT IN (1880 TO 1952

Jim Soper

A glorious summer's day in 1924 with Leeds-built tram 116 en route to Roundhay Park. Passengers are boarding the tram in Street Lane at Moortown Corner and on the platform dash is an advertisement for the Test Match at Headingley between England and South Africa. The fare from Briggate to the Cricket Ground was 2d. and the match was held from 14 to 16 July. England won. This view was copied from a damaged postcard. *W. Taylor, Moortown.*

Published by the Leeds Transport Historical Society 2017

A Society for the study and preservation of local passenger transport
Charitable Incorporated Organisation No. 1160466
Registered Address: 17 Church Street, Gildersome, Morley, Leeds, LS27 7AE

Printed by The Amadeus Press,
Cleckheaton. BD19 4TQ

Hardback ISBN 978-0-9510280-8-7
Soft cover ISBN 978-0-9510280-9-4

From 1908 to 1948 the Leeds Tramways Department built over 180 trams at the Kirkstall Road Tramway Works. Car 320 was new in April 1914 and was the typical modern Leeds tram in the period from about 1911 to 1923. The appeal for recruits for the Royal Engineers in the lower saloon window suggests that the tram was about three months old when this photograph was taken. The location is the yard of Kirkstall Road Works. The car was withdrawn in August 1945 and, during its life of thirty one years, travelled about 1,000,000 miles. *Leeds City Tramways.*

INTRODUCTION

Every person sees colours differently and every camera, colour film, and exposure shows different colours for the same view or object. Modern digital cameras also show differing colours depending on the lighting conditions.

This book is an attempt to record for the benefit of future vehicle restorers, replica builders and modellers the colour schemes or liveries of the various public transport vehicles that were seen in Leeds before the introduction of colour films in the early 1950's. It also shows the general reader that Leeds in the late nineteenth and early twentieth century was a colourful place in which to live.

Although one or two attempts have been made to record early railway liveries, as far as we are aware this is the first effort that has been made to give an impression of the colours of public transport vehicles in any city. All are from original black and white postcards, photographs or negatives that have been digitally restored and coloured.

In the case of the horse-drawn buses of the late nineteenth century the LTHS has several very good photographs of the vehicles, but has no idea of their colours. We know that Coates' Beeston Hill buses were blue, but that is all. Of the several photographs seen, they were in different styles but probably all in a similar blue shade. On these early buses, it appears that the coach painter was told the basic colour scheme and then given "carte blanche" to decorate and line them out as he wished. Probably some of the smaller proprietors had no "standard" livery and left it to the coach painter to produce an attractive colour scheme for their vehicles.

In the case of the Leeds Tramways Company and Leeds City Tramways trams and buses we have much more accurate information. From the commencement of the horse trams in 1871 we know that they were painted in chocolate, primrose and white with bright red decoration and these basic colours with many variations were used on the electric trams and buses until 1925. We are confident the shades of these colours on Leeds horse car 107 and electric car 399 at the National Tramway Museum, Crich, Derbyshire, revealed when the original paintwork was rubbed down and subjected to Spectrometer tests, are "spot on" regarding accuracy. In this publication, we have tried to show some of the many variations in this livery.

We are less certain of the precise colour of the Roundhay Electric Tramway cars. According to people who remembered them they were painted reddish brown, but a model seen of one of the cars, believed to be contemporary, shows they had a greater red content than brown.

The royal blue colour scheme of the first Leeds Corporation electric cars was inspired by the colours of the new electric trams in Bristol, which Leeds councillors inspected in February 1896. Unfortunately, the blue soon darkened and looked dirty in the Leeds atmosphere and in 1899 the City Council decided to go back to the old Leeds Tramways Company livery.

Leeds Tramways General Manager, John Baillie Hamilton, was happy with the chocolate, primrose and white colour scheme, but his successor, William Chamberlain, in 1925 decided to make his mark by the adoption of a new modern Princess Blue and white colour scheme inspired by that in use on the Sheffield and Bradford tramways. Princess Blue was a dark blue, but had more of a blue content than the blue used on the Sheffield cars. It was found that the white could not be varnished without giving a streaky yellow effect and varnish was added to the white, giving an off white or pale ivory effect which quickly yellowed to cream. The shade of blue as used on Leeds car 345 at the National Tramway Museum is considered by the LTHS to be 100% accurate.

A change of General Manager in 1932 when William Vane Morland arrived from Walsall resulted in another livery alteration. He tried to introduce the Walsall livery of turquoise blue and cream and was successful for the buses, but it was not liked on the trams and he had to revert to Princess Blue. The appearance of the "Middleton Bogies" and "Lance Corporal" cars in 1933 and 1935 gave Vane Morland the opportunity to introduce an electric blue livery. This was vaguely the same as Walsall blue and had a turquoise content and, although there are three original colour photographs and remembered by the writer and others, in the absence of any original paint samples we have had difficulty in trying to recreate it. We cannot guarantee that it is 100% accurate.

During the Second World War, all the Leeds buses were painted in a very drab khaki grey livery and many of the trams a slightly less drab khaki green. Post war the buses had a similarly drab blue grey livery, the idea of the bus Rolling stock engineer, Tom Parkinson. The tram Princess Blue and white livery was subjected to several alterations during this period.

The electric blue and Princess Blue liveries lasted until 1948 when a new tramway rolling stock engineer, Victor Matterface, arrived from London. He was responsible for the acquisition of second hand cars from Southampton and the 90 ex-London Transport Feltham cars. He was also responsible for the many livery changes from 1948 to 1952 including the adoption of the red livery for trams and green for buses in 1950. Some of these livery variations, which escaped the colour film, are included in this book.

The writer has coloured the photographs, assisted by his daughter, Helen, an art teacher. She advised on the background colours. The writers' grand daughter, Catherine, also helped with the colouring.

Jim Soper, Leeds Transport Historical Society, June 2017.

Coates' Beeston Hill bus at the Royal Hotel, Briggate, terminus about 1890. Charlie Coates, a farmer at Swillington, was a staunch Conservative. His buses were blue, but in different styles. *D.Hunt.*

Coates' bus turning the corner from Beeston Road into the terminus at Lady Pit Street about 1890. Three white horses can be seen waiting to bring another bus to Leeds. *D.Hunt.*

Eli Spurdens ran buses mainly in the Burley Road and Cardigan Road area.   His bus is rounding the corner from City Square into West Bar, (Boar Lane). The new Post Office is under construction in the background with on the right the old Post Office and the corner of the Royal Exchange building. In an interview in 1944, Spurdens said that his buses were painted vermilion and primrose.   *D.Hunt.*

This was the last horse bus to Seacroft, which ran at the end of 1904. Walter Dobson of the Old Red Lion Inn, Whinmoor, ran the bus for the last four years of its existence and his bus appears to have been formerly used by Walker Bros. of Chapeltown Road, whose buses were painted in a tartan livery. The boy was the conductor and he also stood at the horses' heads to steady the vehicle.   *Anon.*

This was almost certainly the last horse bus to leave Kirkstall Road Works for Farnley in 1911. The clue is the blackened hooves of the horses. It was a Leeds practice to black the hooves of horses making their last journey. Afterwards they went to the knacker's yard for slaughter.   The bus was preserved at the former Hunslet Depot tram stables until 1926 when it and a couple of horse trams were destroyed on the instructions of a new General Manager, William Chamberlain.   *L.C.T.*

In 1954, when the writer asked the daughter of James Gill the colours of the bus used by her father and the opposition bus run by Thomas Bean, she could not remember. There was probably no "standard" livery and it was left to the coach painter to determine the colours. On 1 June 1905 Gill and Bean ran the last buses to Hunslet Carr, "fully 500 people" being present. This is Gill's bus and we have "painted" it in maroon, a popular colour. "Johnnie on the Road" was the nick-name of the driver. *J.Gill.*

An early view of Starbuck-built horse car 25 outside Headingley tram depot about 1880. Note the cat ladder access to the upper deck. *Anon.*

A wet day about 1890 with a rebuilt horse car at the "Queen Inn", Chapeltown tram terminus. Thanks mainly to its chairman, William Turton, the Leeds Tramways Company had some very fine horses and always tried to match its horses for colour. Here are three greys with the leader a dapple grey. *Anon.*

When horses reached the end of their working life they were transferred to the short York Road tram route from Duncan Street to the Woodpecker Junction. This poor tired horse has blackened hooves indicating that it was making its last journey. The tram is car No.1, one of three 16-seat Starbuck cars new in 1888. From the left are the driver, an inspector, unnamed, who appears on several photographs of the period, (see pages 10 and 11) and the conductor. *Anon.*

Eades Reversible car 58 at the Woodman Inn, Headingley, about 1890. *Anon .*

Tram engine No.4 built by Leeds firm Kitson & Co. and trailer 71 at Headingley Oak on 10 May 1888. Trailers, Nos.71-73, built by the Ashbury Railway and Carriage Company, Manchester, were the most unpopular and claustrophobic trams in the Leeds Tramways Company fleet. The ceiling height in the upper saloon was a maximum of 5ft.3in. in the centre and 4ft. 9in. at the perimeter.
Godfrey Bingley, Leeds University Collection.

The same tram engine as above but after an overhaul and rebuild in 1891. The newly repainted trailer was supplied by G.F. Milnes in 1889. The location is the yard of Wellington Bridge Depot. The building was open sided and later used by the Leeds Tramways Permanent Way Department. Much later it was the site of the Yorkshire Post Offices, built in 1970 and demolished in 2014. *Anon.*

Kitson engine 9 and Ashbury trailer 59 at the Crown Hotel, New Wortley, about 1890.   *Anon.*

1892 with a very dirty tram engine 24, built by Thomas Green & Sons of Leeds, contrasting with a newly repainted Milnes trailer 41 at Wortley terminus. The driver is James Wade, later the foreman at Wellington Bridge Depot.   *Late J.Wade.*

The Roundhay Electric Tramway was the first tramway in the country to be operated using overhead electric wires. It ran from 1891 to 1896 between Sheepscar and Horse Shoe Corner (later known as Oakwood) and along Harehills Road to Beckett Street. This is one of the six cars (75-80) built by John Stephenson & Co. of New York. It is at Horse Shoe Corner at the entrance to Roundhay Park.   *Anon.*

Car 79 at Beckett Street Depot. On the step is I.E. Winslow, the Manager of the tramway.   *W. Nichols.*

Kirkstall Abbey terminus with Greenwood & Batley car 6 about 1897. *Anon.*

The opposite end of the line at Roundhay Park, Canal Gardens, with car 13. *Anon.*

A big event in the history of Leeds tramways. The opening of the electric tramway from Roundhay to Kirkstall at 12 noon on 29 July 1897, an all-male event. Greenwood and Batley cars 1 and 2, together with virtually all members of the Corporation and some members of other local authorities, posed for a photograph. The Tramways Manager, William Wharam, with top hat, is the tall man in the centre of the picture (below the gas lamp) and fifth from the left wearing a bowler hat is John Burbridge, the Chief Electrical Engineer. The writer's maternal grandfather, Richard Atkinson, was a joiner working on some new houses in Harehills Avenue and witnessed the procession in Roundhay Road. *Anon.*

Ex-trailer car 128 at Meanwood terminus about 1901. *A.K.Terry.*

Car 85 was one of 14 B.T-H. cars that were rejected by Leeds Corporation in 1899 as being "not in accordance with the specification" having curved top windows instead of "tudor arch" i.e. pointed tops, see illustration below. Cars 143-154 were delivered and returned to B.T-H., but two car bodies were retained and numbered 85 and 90. 85 had track brakes and powerful motors and is ascending the steepest part of Beeston Hill, 1 in 11. The year is 1906.   *Phototype Company.*

The Rodley tramway was opened in 1906 and had the steepest hill on the Leeds tramway system - 1 in 8 Whitecote Hill. B.T-H. car 151 (a replacement for the rejected 151) was well equipped with Westinghouse Newall track brakes. It was photographed at Rodley terminus shortly after the tramway opened. In the left background is the Leeds and Liverpool Canal.   *Phototype Company.*

B.T-H. car 153 at the York Road tram terminus at Halton Dial at the junction of the York and Selby Roads. The former toll house is in the right background. It was demolished in 1929 to make way for the widening of York Road into a dual carriageway and tramway reservation. The distant clock tower of Seacroft Hospital is just visible on the left hand side of the picture. *W. Bramley.*

Looking down Harehills Road to the Harehills tram terminus in Roundhay Road with B.T-H. car 157 bound for Beeston and, waiting to turn on the crossover, 1902 Brush car 86. This photograph was taken in 1906 and a few years later the terrace houses on the left were converted into a parade of shops known as Harehills Parade, which still exists. *Phototype Company.*

Sunshine and shadows in Cardigan Road with B.T-H. car 175 bound for Balm Road.   The year – about 1907.
W. & T. Gaines /LTHS.

Car 49 was a "one-off". It was a Brill Convertible car purchased in 1900. It ran until 1913 and was confined to the lightly used Corn Exchange-Whitehall Road tram route. This 1911 photograph also shows one of the new trackless cars, 504, and behind B.T-H. car 170.
Anon.

Most of the B.T-H. cars received top covers in 1912, but the design was such that when it rained, and the driver applied the brakes, the rain fell directly from the short canopy onto the driver. They were not popular and very quickly nick-named "bathing vans". Car 85 was photographed in Victoria Road shortly after receiving its top cover. *Leeds City Tramways.*

The Greenwood & Batley cars were top-covered in 1908; car 8 was the first on 11 March. In 1913 they were fitted with platform vestibules. Car 8 is at Roundhay Park waiting to return to Horsforth. *Anon.*

When new the cars built by the Dick, Kerr Company of Preston in 1901, were painted in an overall primrose and white livery. The dashes soon looked dirty and most were repainted in chocolate within about two years. Car 259 is at the New Inn, Wortley terminus.   *A.K.Terry.*

Car 264 at Whingate in 1901.   *A.K.Terry.*

To mark the end of the Boer War in 1902 the Leeds Tramways Department hastily produced this illuminated tram. It was the idea of John Burbridge, the Chief Electrical Engineer, and was stated to be the first illuminated tramcar in the U.K. Leeds' example was soon followed by other authorities to mark the Coronation of Edward VII later in the year. Car 231 had 800 crimson, green and violet bulbs and the destination blinds revolved showing LADYSMITH, MAFEKING, KIMBERLEY and PRETORIA. The word "PEACE" was on a frosted ground and the "gorgeous sight" ran from 1 to 8 June 1902. *Anon.*

Lower Briggate, 1906 with Dick,Kerr car 185 and 1904 Brush car 35. *W.& T.Gaines/A.K.Terry.*

Car 253 at Lower Wortley terminus about 1905. It is still in its original 1901 style livery, but the dashes have been repainted chocolate. The clue is the white corner pillars, other cars in Leeds having red corners. When fully repainted, often having been top covered for some time, the corner pillars on these cars were repainted red. It seems as if the local children had strict instructions to keep out of the photograph.   *Anon.*

Headingley in 1905 with Dick, Kerr car 223 posed for the photographer.   The historic Shire oak fell down on 26 May 1941.   *Phototype Company.*

The Woodpecker Junction in 1905 with newly top covered cars 274 and 277. The Woodpecker Inn was at the bottom of York Road and from its construction by 1817 to demolition in 1939 was a prominent landmark in Leeds. It was replaced on the opposite side of the road by a new building, bombed during the war, rebuilt and eventually demolished in 1990 to make way for the Leeds Inner Ring Road. There is currently a flyover at this point, but in the leisurely days of 1905 it was possible for a man with one leg to walk across the junction without hindrance. *T.Baker.*

Car 211 at the Fleece Hotel, the Horsforth tram terminus, shortly after the tram route was opened in 1906. In 1909 the tramway was extended to Rawdon, Yeadon and Guiseley and later still to the White Cross Inn at Guiseley forming a connection with the Otley and Burley trackless routes. *H. Graham Glen.*

Dick, Kerr car 246 in Briggate 1908. The date was 7 July, an occasion when King Edward VII and Queen Alexandra visited Leeds to open Leeds University. Much of the route from Harewood House to the University was lined with flags, flowers and triumphal arches. Some trams were decorated for the event.   *Phototype Company.*

B.T-H. car 170 appears to have been decorated for the King's visit by the staff at Headingley Depot. They had some flags and bunting, but were short of flowers. There were some Christmas decorations inside the tram, but much of the external decoration was of tree leaves. The photograph is taken outside the depot at the Headingley tram terminus.   It seems unlikely that the tram would have run in passenger service in this condition.   *Anon.*

Dick, Kerr car 207 in Otley Road, Far Headingley, shortly after the tramway was extended to West Park in 1908. It is on a single track at a pinch point just above Glen Road on the right. Otley Road was widened in early 1910 and the track doubled. The tram is on its way to Chapeltown. *W.& T.Gaines.*

Duncan Street with the Corn Exchange as a backdrop about 1910. Dick, Kerr car 267 is on its way to Waterloo Lane at Bramley and passing is West Riding tram 50 from Wakefield. *C.R.Pickard/A.K.Terry.*

The 2 July 1911 was a big day in the history of Morley. The first tram was seen at Morley Bottoms and it attracted a great deal of local interest. It was a trial car and the driver was John Burbridge, the Chief Tramways Electrical Engineer. Burbridge was formerly the Manager of the Roundhay Electric Tramway and stated by his daughters to be a kind and courteous man. He drove the first electric car in Leeds and all the trial cars on the numerous new tram routes, until his retirement in 1926. See also page 66. *Anon.*

On 1 January 1912 a tramway extension was opened from the Fountain Inn, Morley, to Bruntcliffe. Dick, Kerr car 248 is at the terminus shortly after the tramway was instituted. *Anon.*

Dick, Kerr car 240 at the old West Park terminus about 1909, before the route was extended about 50 yards further up Otley Road.   *Anon.*

In 1914 Dick, Kerr car 272 was decorated as a Recruiting Car for the War Effort. In red white and blue it had a lot of blue muslin, with red frills, but not many lamps. It ran over the whole of the tramway system.   *Anon.*

THE 1902 BRUSH CARS (50 CARS)

The Brush cars were delivered as open top cars with reversed staircases and carried fleet numbers vacated by recently withdrawn horse trams. 91 and 47 were photographed soon after delivery at Headingley Depot.   *Anon.*

Brush car 51 was fitted with an experimental top cover, which it had from 1907 to 1921.   It was photographed at the Queen's Arms, Chapeltown terminus, soon after the cover was fitted.   *Anon.*

Beeston terminus about 1905 with newly top covered car 112. The little girl is wearing a very large hat - her mother's?   *J.William Wood, Beeston.*

Oakwood Clock with Brush car 48 shortly after the Clock was moved from the Central Market in 1913. The fine building in the background is the "new" entrance to Roundhay Park, built in 1889 and demolished in 1937. It served as a waiting room, toilets, battery room for electric cars etc.   *L.C.T.*

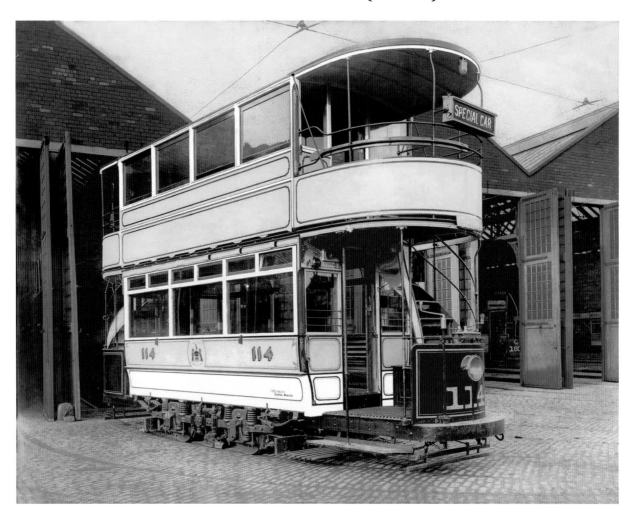

A brand new Brush-built car 114 at Kirkstall Road Works. It looks immaculate and was supplied as a top covered car. Most of the 1904 cars occupied fleet numbers vacated by steam car trailers.   *Anon.*

Brush car 66 on the Harehills Avenue spur, Chapeltown Road, the Reginald Terrace terminus.   *Anon.*

A threatening sky at Cardigan Road terminus with Brush car 72.   *Anon.*

Car 64 at Rothwell tram terminus soon after the tram route was opened in 1905. Note the macadam road surface. Whereas Leeds Corporation paved its new tramways with granite setts, the Wakefield and District Light Railways Company, which built the Rothwell and Wakefield lines, used the much cheaper alternative. It was a false economy as there were many complaints and only two or three years after completion the line between Leeds and Wakefield was described as "very bumpy". When the tramway was abandoned in 1932 it was in an atrocious condition.   *Phototype Company.*

On 26 May 1909, there were several first trams to Rawdon mainly using new Leeds-built cars of the 115-126 series. Car 122 was reserved for the Rawdon councillors and their wives and to the left of the group is a Leeds Tramways Inspector. The tram entered normal passenger service the following day. The photograph appears to be taken at Rawdon cross roads. See also page 65. *J.K.S. Rawdon.*

Leeds-built car 117 in Woodhouse Lane at Hyde Park Corner in 1913. It is en route to Chapeltown.
C.R. Pickard/A.K.Terry.

An immaculate new Leeds-built car 289 posed for the photographer at Kirkstall Abbey in April 1912.
Leeds City Tramways.

New Road Side, Rawdon, with Leeds-built car 307 on its way to Guiseley. The year is about 1920. *Anon.*

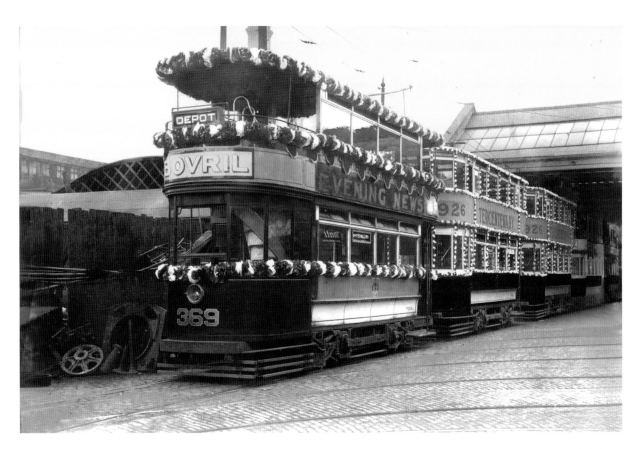

For the Leeds Tercentenary in 1926 car 369 appears to be decorated with bundles of glazed fabric. The new trams behind in the Princess Blue and white livery are cars 401 and 402. They seem to have balls of wool on strings as decoration. Several of the newer cars of this type were similarly decorated. In addition to the above, photographs have been seen of cars 386, 392 and 400.   *Anon.*

Armley Road about 1930 with workmen loading "tippler" car 15 with granite paving setts. The industrial building on the right was the last tramway era building on this photograph to survive. It was demolished from May to July 2016.   The terrace housing disappeared in the 1960's.
Leeds City Tramways/A.K.Terry.

A brand new Ryknield double deck bus at Headingley Golf Club, Adel, in 1906, one of two similar vehicles. The General Manager, J.B. Hamilton, and Chairman of the Tramways Committee, Alderman Smithson, were members of the Golf Club, but following complaints from the public, after a short time the bus terminus was altered to nearby Adel Church. The Ryknield bus was later fitted with a single deck body (see below). The bus driver is dressed in oil skins.   *Phototype Company.*

Until 1913 Shadwell had a horse bus connection with the tramway at Moortown Corner. Greenwood's horse bus ran three times daily. In October 1913, it was replaced by a motor bus service, two vehicles being used one of which was this 40 h.p. Tilling Stevens, U 2379. It had a 24-seat single deck body formerly on Ryknield bus U 327. The bus was short lived and on the outbreak of war in 1914 it was commandeered as an ambulance.   *Leeds City Tramways.*

The other Shadwell motor bus was this splendid double deck Daimler U 2380. This was probably its first journey and it has the local children as passengers. On 5 June 1915, it was taken out of service and converted into a motor derrick. For much of the War Shadwell had an intermittent bus service. *Anon.*

In 1922 Leeds opened a motor bus service to Farnley and the following year six new buses were supplied by Guy Motors Ltd. of Wolverhampton with 16-seat bodies of the "most modern design" built by the Leeds Tramways Department. This sylvan scene shows the bus terminus in Hall Lane, Old Farnley. *C.Haxby, Farnley.*

Although the 20th June 1911 was a fine mid-summer's day, there were not many spectators when the first trackless car, 503, arrived at Farnley Moor Top. The car was supplied by the Railless Electric Traction Company. On the platform is the Lord Mayor of Leeds, Alderman William Middlebrook, M.P. Copied from a postcard, the writer of which was impressed. "What do you think of our cars then? Don't you think we are getting up in the world?" He wrote that the man at the back wearing a bowler hat and bow tie was called Abraham Lee and the man with white beard was a local character nicknamed "Ow'd Tune". See also page 66. *W.Taylor, Bramley.*

The turning circle at Farnley Moor Top about 1912 with trackless car 504. *Anon.*

The trackless car routes from Guiseley to Otley and Burley-in-Wharfedale were opened in 1915 using cars made by David Brown & Sons of Huddersfield to a Bradford City Tramways design.   At first young boys were used as conductors, but in late 1915 were replaced by lady conductors.   *Anon.*

Double deck trackless car 512 in Aire Street, Leeds, on 15 May 1925. The car had a cumbersome Bishop's Front wheel drive, with worm gear steering. To turn from Aire Street into Wellington Street required over 30 revolutions of the steering wheel and accidents were common place.   *Anon.*

In November 1925, new Leeds-built car 400 looked magnificent in its Sheffield style Princess Blue and white livery. Note the absence of bulkheads in the upper saloon and the destination indicators – the only tram in Leeds with this destination arrangement. *Leeds City Tramways.*

There were 185 Chamberlain cars (1-150 and 411-445) built between 1926-1928. Car 134 was one of 75 (cars 76-150) built by the English Electric Company of Preston. *Leeds City Tramways.*

Chamberlain car 5, one of 75 cars (1-75) built by the Brush Electrical Engineering Company of Loughborough. It is at the entrance to Headingley Depot about 1927.   *Leeds City Tramways.*

Stanningley Bottom about 1928 with a newly repainted Leeds-built tram 378. From 1909-1918 dual gauge tramcars ran between Leeds and Bradford. The tapered tracks are still in position, but there is a gap of about three feet between the Leeds and Bradford rails.   *Matthews, Bradford.*

City Square about 1928 with Chamberlain car 83. Prominent in the centre of the picture is the Royal Exchange building. On the left is Mill Hill Chapel and the right the Queens Hotel. *C.R.Pickard/ A.K.Terry.*

Kirkstall Abbey terminus February 1930 with a new Leeds-built Horsfield car 151. *L.C.T.*

In 1931 and 1932 Leeds took delivery of 100 Horsfield cars, (155-254), from the Brush Electrical Engineering Co., Loughborough. The first of the batch is pictured at the Brush Works. *Brush.*

Tingley tram terminus, Morley, with Horsfield car 172. The year: about 1934 shortly before the tram route closed. Tingley Bar fish and chip shop, on the corner, was there in 1920 and was still in business in 2017.   *Morley and District Historical Society.*

Lower Wortley terminus on 23 July 1939 with Chamberlain car 14. W.A. Camwell's Morris car is on the right. He drove over several Leeds tram routes on that day. *W.A. Camwell/National Tramway Museum.*

The new Lawnswood tram terminus on 23 July 1939 with Chamberlain car 67 and Horsfield 205. The covered rails of the old terminus are in the foreground. *W.A. Camwell/National Tramway Museum.*

Hawksworth Road tram terminus on 23 July 1939 with Leeds-built Chamberlain car 415. The former crossover and rails to Guiseley, abandoned in 1934, can be seen in the foreground.
W.A. Camwell/National Tramway Museum.

Kirkstall Abbey terminus with car 343 on 23 July 1939. It was newly totally enclosed or "converted" from an open balcony car. Camwell's Morris 8, EOX 211, is parked in the background.
W.A.Camwell/National Tramway Museum.

This Karrier WL6/2, No.53, UM 8073, was the first six-wheeler bus to be purchased by the Leeds Tramways Department. It was new in 1927 and built by Charles H. Roe Ltd. of Cross Gates. *C.H. Roe Ltd.*

From 1926 to 1932 the Leeds buses were painted in the Princess Blue and white livery. This Leyland Titan TD1, 107, was one of the last. *Leyland Motors Ltd.*

In 1932 a Walsall turquoise blue livery was introduced. The livery was said to "not look right" on the trams. They appeared green. Five Chamberlains and one Horsfield car received the livery. The L.T.H.S. has "repainted" a Chamberlain car, car 39, the only one of its type with track brakes.   *L.C.T.*

New Dennis Lance 125 in Walsall blue and white in 1932. It is in Queenswood Drive.   *Charles H. Roe.*

Maudslay buses 9 and 10 were the only second hand buses to be purchased by the Leeds Transport Department. Acquired on 23 July 1935 they had 32-seat bodies and ran for under three years. They were ex-H. V. Barker of Britannia Garage, Morley, and this is number 10.   *Leeds City Transport.*

The bus rolling stock engineer, Tom Parkinson, was concerned that the white on the buses soon looked dirty and in 1935 the new "art deco" style A.E.C. Regent streamlined bus 200 received pale blue instead of white. It was exhibited at the Commercial Motor Show in 1935.   Although, until 1938, most subsequent new buses had white bands, some, including repaints, had pale blue or greyish blue. *A.E.C.*

New Middleton Bogie trams to his design gave Vane Morland the opportunity to introduce a Walsall style livery for the new cars. Electric blue had a turquoise content but differed from Walsall blue. 255 was the prototype Middleton Bogie and is in Middleton Woods with members of the Tramways, Light Railways and Transport Association in June 1933. Chromium plate was fashionable in the 1930's and an "art deco" feature. Two strips were placed above the bumpers on 255 and the Brush-built cars 256-263. They were purely decorative, but soon rusted and had to be painted over. They were all removed in the late 1940's.   *Yorkshire Observer.*

An English Electric Company–built Middeton Bogie passing Chamberlain car 34 in Duncan Street in 1939. The chromium-plated strips were omitted on these cars (264-271).   *Anon.*

brand-new "Lance Corporal" 272 looked splendid in its electric blue livery. With ...llo revolving seats, the three "Lance Corporals", with the Middleton Bogies, both ...birds", were for many years the most popular Leeds trams.   *Leeds City Transport.*

All the three ex-London HR/2 cars (277-279) purchased in 1939 were painted in the electric blue and white livery.   This view shows 278 in wartime condition with headlamp masks and white bumpers. The location is Street Lane, Moortown, and the date about 1945.   *M.J. O'Connor.*

At the outbreak of war, to meet black-out regulations, all the pre-1928 trams had projections, i.e. bumpers and platform steps painted white and a broad white band painted on the dashes. Headlamp masks were fitted later. The old open balcony trams still in service including 297, seen as a shunter outside Swinegate Depot, received this treatment. On the balcony, on the right is Brian Render and in the centre, Jim Wade, the foreman at Swinegate Depot. The date 25 October 1942. *Stuart Pickford.*

Cars 316 and 293 were withdrawn in 1942 and burned in Lowfields Road Yard on 16 November 1945.
W.D.Wilson.

The trams purchased from Hull Corporation in 1942, cars 446-477, replaced the open balcony cars seen on the previous page. The ex-Hulls were painted in a khaki green livery. The windows were covered in anti-blast netting glued to the glass with a central clear portion. When newly painted they looked quite smart. Car 448 is at Hunslet terminus. *Eric Thornton.*

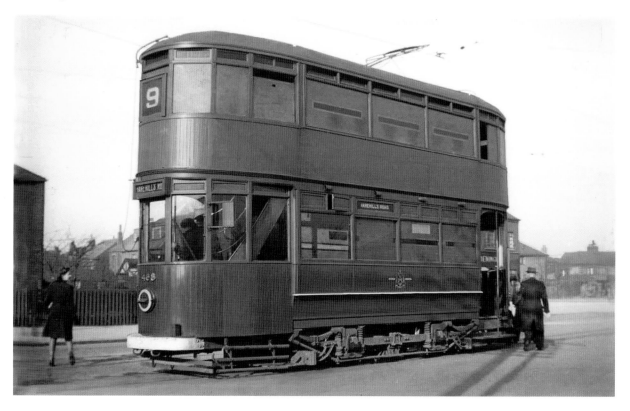

The diamond shape vision panels in the window netting were difficult to see through, especially at night, and the later ex-Hull cars, and many other trams, had a narrow clear vision slot. Car 468 is at Dewsbury Road terminus in February 1943. *M.J.O'Connor.*

From 1942 to 1944 many of the Hamilton enclosed cars (370-410) and Chamberlains were repainted in khaki with a narrow white band on the dash. Car 399 is at Easterly Road, Harehills, on 6 May 1946. *A.K.Terry.*

This 27 February 1943 picture by Brian Render is the best we have been able to find of a Horsfield car newly repainted in khaki. It was "chopped off" at the bumper and we have had to digitally "paint" the lifeguards, track and legs of the people on the photograph. On the right is Jim Wade, foreman at Swinegate Depot. Brian "arranged" the destination blind. The last tram ran to Pudsey in 1938. *G.B.R.*

Leeds Tramways Department continued to paint trams in Princess Blue and white until the paint was in short supply in 1942. Chamberlain car 149 was painted in a simplified version of the livery in September of that year. It had a narrow white band, blue rocker panels and pale blue lining on the upper and lower panelling. Location Lawnswood terminus, September 1942. *Ted Wurm.*

Car 351 was one of only two "Converts" (351 and 369) painted in this version of the Princess Blue and white livery. It is on the then relatively new Burley Mills siding in Kirkstall Road. The date: 15 August 1944. *W.D.Wilson/L.T.H.S.*

In 1943 a new tram appeared in Leeds. It was a replacement for Chamberlain 104 destroyed by fire on 3 July 1942. Known as the "Austerity Car" it entered service in December 1943. It was painted in a dove grey and white colour scheme with a sky blue beading above the lower white band. It was given the nick name "Grey Lady". *Leeds City Transport.*

In 1945, the Hull tramways system was abandoned and the second batch of Hull trams (478-487) was delivered to Leeds. They entered service in the Princess Blue and white livery. Car 485 was photographed at Hunslet terminus in 1946. The rails to the former Hunslet tram depot were removed soon after this photograph was taken. *A.D.Packer.*

During the war all the buses in Leeds were painted in this most depressing khaki grey livery. This is one of the "HUM" registered A.E.C. Regents, the most modern buses in Leeds at the time. It is hauling a gas producer trailer.   *Leeds City Transport.*

1932 vintage A.E.C. Regal 29 in the khaki grey livery. It is at the Prospect Hotel, Morley, about 1944. *Anon.*

From 1946 to 1950 this rather uninspiring blue livery was used for the Leeds buses. It soon looked drab and was the idea of Tom Parkinson, the bus rolling stock engineer. He was obsessed with maintenance costs and was not interested in attracting passengers on to the buses. A.E.C. Regent 289 is at Christ Church, Armley Ridge Road, and the date 29 May 1950. *W.D.Wilson/L.T.H.S.*

The Crossleys, 702-721, new in 1949, were painted in the two shades of blue livery. The upper blue band improved the appearance of the livery. The bus is at East End Park on 13 May 1950.
W.D.Wilson/L.T.H.S.

To the writer this is the typical Leeds tram, which he rode on daily to and from school from 1944 to 1950. It is a 1926 Leeds-built Chamberlain car on an EMB Pivotal truck.   It is pictured outside Chapeltown Depot and was photographed by Bob Parr on 3 May 1949.   Although there is a Horsfield car in the depot yard, more Chamberlains ran from the depot than Horsfields.   *R.B.Parr.*

Ex-Manchester Pilcher car 287 (later renumbered 280) looked smart when newly repainted in March 1948. It was the only Pilcher to receive this livery. It is outside Headingley Depot.   *R.Brook/L.T.H.S.*

A typical August 1949 view of Leeds-built car 374 in Meadow Lane.   *R.F.Mack.*

Ex-Hull car 473 never recovered from this accident in Swinegate Depot on 22 September 1949. It was burned on 16 May the following year. Not surprisingly the driver was sacked. On the right is one of five Converted cars that were cut down as single deckers from May 1949 to January 1950 and used as cleaner's cars in Swinegate Depot. They were positioned between tracks 15 and 16 and painted in red oxide with large white numerals centrally on the waist panels (1 to 5). This is No.1 ex-348.
Leeds City Transport.

Victor J. Matterface took up the post of the Leeds Tramway Rolling Stock Engineer on 1 May 1948. Changes to the rolling stock were soon apparent. His first action was to adopt a simplified livery. The white bands on the Horsfield cars disappeared and were replaced by Princess Blue. Four Horsfield cars, 173, 197, 199 and 254, appeared in this livery. Donald Wilson took this photograph at Easterly Road on 27 July 1948 about a fortnight after car 254 had been repainted. *W.D.Wilson/L.T.H.S.*

The Middleton bogies lost their white bands and were in a different shade of blue. 258 is at Whingate terminus on an L.R.T.L. tour on 24 October 1948. John Price is on the platform. *W.D.Wilson/L.T.H.S.*

In September 1948, new car 276 looked smart in its Matterface light turquoise blue and white livery. It had a silver roof, London Transport style Gill Sans numerals and a new "LEEDS CITY TRANSPORT" insignia on the side panels. On the platform is the warden of Kirkstall Road Tramway Works.   *L.C.T.*

Ex-London Transport HR/2, 277, was painted in Matterface light blue and was the first Leeds tram to receive Gill Sans numerals, but the "7s" were not available and differed from those on other cars. In place of white it had yellowish cream window surrounds which soon looked scruffy and was the only tram to receive this colour. At Middleton, the short man wearing a hat to the left of 277 is Bob Parr, the energetic and enthusiastic first Chairman of the Tramway Museum Society.   *R. Brook/ L.T.H.S.*

Middleton Bogie 265 on an L.R.T.L. tour, 24 October 1948. It is at the Gelderd Road end of the Lowfields Road football siding. It was one of seven Middleton Bogies painted in this livery (with minor variations). The cars were 262, 265-269 and 271. A youth is admiring the new "LEEDS CITY TRANSPORT" insignia, which only appeared on these cars and new car 276. That on 269 was painted in red.

Anon.

With the exception of car 280 (ex-287), all the other ex-Manchester Pilcher cars, 281-286, were painted in Matterface light blue with silver roofs. This photograph was taken by Bob Mack on the Victoria Road spur in July 1950. There are no "good" colour photographs of this livery and at a meeting of LTHS members this view was stated to be an accurate representation of the colour. *R.F.Mack.*

Only two Horsfield cars, 164 and 208, were painted in Matterface light turquoise blue. 164 is in New Briggate and about to enter North Street in 1948. 158 in the Princess Blue and white livery is in the background.

R.F.Mack.

Ex-Southampton car 290 looked smart in City Square when "new" in 1949. It was painted in Southampton and the interior woodwork was bright green. However, like all trams in this livery it soon looked dirty in the Leeds atmosphere and was repainted after two years.

R. Brook/L.T.H.S.

The shade difference between the earlier electric blue livery and Matterface light turquoise blue was not great, but for some unknown reason, electric blue "weathered" much better than the Matterface colour. When "Lance Corporal" 272 was repainted in May 1949, William Vane Morland, the General Manager, insisted that it be done in electric blue, the colour he had introduced in 1933. It was the last tram to be painted in electric blue. Matterface had "modernised" the car by recessing the headlamps and using Gill Sans numerals. The location is Gipton terminus and date 15 August 1949. *W.D.Wilson/L.T.H.S.*

Although in July 1948 this livery looked reasonably smart when new, it was a disaster. It weathered badly and quickly looked scruffy. It was soon nicknamed "black and white". *A.D.Packer.*

Leeds-built car 399 was painted in a similar livery to Horsfield car 189 on the previous page, but had brown indicators. The location is Beeston terminus and Roy Brook took this fine photograph on 8 October 1950 on an L.R.T.L. tour. The tour car was Horsfield 153 seen behind, and then newly repainted in an experimental all red livery. 153 is alas no more, but 399 runs regularly at the National Tramway Museum at Crich in Derbyshire. *R.Brook/L.T.H.S.*

Another tram which has been preserved for posterity is ex-Hull car 446 seen here in Sovereign Street on an Elland Road football special on 3 March 1951. Behind is a Leeds-built car of the 370-410 series. As Hull car 132, 446 is on display at "Streetlife", the Hull Museum of Transport. *Author.*

Four of the ex-Hull cars, 467, 481, 485 and 486, survived long enough to be repainted in the Matterface royal blue livery and they looked smart. The date is 20 May 1950 and location, North Street. *Author.*

Another tram which has been preserved for posterity at the National Tramway Museum is Horsfield car 180, photographed at the Park Gates at the top of Beeston Hill on 2 June 1952. It is in the Matterface royal blue livery. *Author.*

An L.R.T.L. tour in April 1950 on ex-London Feltham 2099, a tram which had proved very popular with the public. The "key" person on the photograph is an enthusiastic Londoner, the Tramway Rolling Stock Engineer, Victor Matterface, sitting on the tram rail on the extreme left.   Matterface was responsible for persuading the Leeds Transport Committee to purchase 90 Felthams from London, and also trams from Southampton.   He was also instrumental in changing the livery of the trams from blue to the London colour red, and the buses from blue to green.   *R.Brook/L.T.H.S.*

Middleton Bogie 255 in electric blue, an accurate representation of the colour, according to L.T.H.S. members who remembered it, passing 269 in a new "Mexican vermilion and dirty buff" livery, emerging from Hunslet Lane in July 1950.   *R.Brook/L.T.H.S.*

In June 1950, beginning with the "JUG" series of A.E.C. Regent III, 401-415, the first Leeds buses appeared in a green livery. Six of the first twenty, 403, 410, 412, 413, 416, and 419 had a red band above the lower saloon windows. The red band was short lived and lasted for a few weeks only. 413 is pictured in Wellington Street. It is returning from Guiseley on service 71, a bus route that was discontinued in 1955.   *W.D.Wilson/ L.T.H.S.*

Ex-Manchester Pilcher car 283 was a tram which avoided the colour film. In August 1952, it was repainted in an overall unlined red livery. Roy Brook took this photograph at the end of the track at Hunslet looking down the A639, Pontefract Road.   *R.Brook/ L.T.H.S.*

in September 1950 Horsfield car 153 was the first car of its type to appear in a red livery. It was used on an L.R.T.L. tour to Beeston on 8 October 1950. Holding a Kodak Brownie box camera and stepping on to the pavement is a younger version of the author. Behind is Ian Smith. *R.Brook/L.T.H.S.*

This livery marked the end of Victor Matterface as Rolling Stock Engineer. It was not liked by the Transport Committee and Tom Parkinson took his place. The Leeds trams became less interesting. The location is Elland Road terminus and date 31 May 1952, 219's first day in red and green. *Author.*

Many of the illustrations in this book are copied from old postcards some of which are faded, damaged or incomplete and a great deal of work was required to get them into a fit state to be coloured.   This is the faded view of the special tram for Rawdon councillors. See page 28.

In the decade before the First World War, enterprising photographers set up their cameras and tripods at a tram terminus and photographed every tram and crew that came along. Probably no more than half a dozen copies of each postcard were produced.   This is a typical yellowed and faded postcard, sent from Hyde Park Corner Post Office on 20 June 1906. The left hand corner is creased and the tram and unusually the conductor are incomplete. The missing detail i.e. the tram lifeguard, roof, trolley, conductor's legs, road, building etc. have been digitally painted on to the coloured illustration – a very time consuming exercise. The name of the conductor was J. Knowles. See page 27.

This 1911 postcard of the first trackless car to Farnley is showing its age. On the coloured illustration the lettering has been removed, trolleys and overhead wires added, an attempt made to sort out the blurring in the right hand corner of the postcard, and the telegraph pole removed. See page 33.

This image on this postcard of the first trial car to Morley in 1911 has almost faded away. The card, however, was in good condition and it was not too difficult to revive. See page 22.